What happens when Volcanoes Erupt?

Daphne Butler

SIMON & SCHUSTER
YOUNG BOOKS

This book was conceived for
Simon & Schuster Young Books by
Globe Enterprises of Nantwich, Cheshire

Design: SPL Design
Photographs: ZEFA

First published in Great Britain in 1993
by Simon & Schuster Young Books
Campus 400, Maylands Avenue
Hemel Hempstead, Herts HP2 7EZ

© 1993 Globe Enterprises

All rights reserved

Printed and bound in Singapore
by Kim Hup Lee Printing Co Pte Ltd

A catalogue record for this book is available
from the British Library
ISBN 0 7500 1296 X

Contents

Once long, long ago

Long ago when the Earth was a new planet, it was not like today.

It was not a good place to be. There were no animals, plants or trees, just a dry, lifeless landscape.

Boiling rock

Even so the Earth was not still.
Under the thin crust, boiling rock
was churning around.

Often it would break through
the surface and pour out across
the land.

Millions of years

Millions of years went by, the land became steady and more solid. Rain fell and made the seas, weathering the rocks, making soil.

Life began. The soil was rich.
Eventually the world came to look
the way it does today.

Volcanoes

There are still places in the world where mountains suddenly explode. Places where dust and gas and liquid rock pour out over the land.

We call the liquid rock, lava, and
we call the mountains, volcanoes.
People study volcanoes so they
can learn more about the Earth.

13

Living with volcanoes

People who live near volcanoes can never be sure what will happen. Sometimes there are earthquakes as the rocks shift and settle.

Sometimes dust and ash pour into
the air settling on houses and
burying them.

Volcano scientists try to warn
people when to leave their homes.
If they stay, they too will be buried.   15

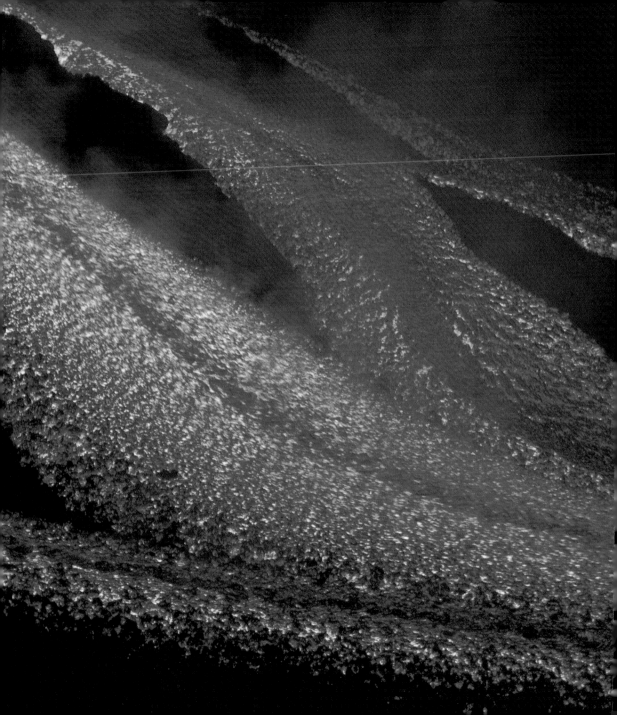

Flowing lava

Lava flows down mountains in rivers, finding the easiest way.

Cooling, it becomes slower. Later, it will become solid rock.

Cone shapes

As a volcano erupts, it grows higher, building up a cone. Old volcanoes can be very beautiful because of their perfect shape.

On top, there is a valley called
a crater where holes may lead
inside the volcano. Sometimes, the
crater smokes.

Inside a crater

The inside of a crater can be a dangerous place.

The sides are steep and the ground hot. There are smelly fumes and sometimes lakes of fresh lava.

Aging volcanoes

When the rocks become steadier, volcanoes stop erupting.
The land cools, the rocks weather and plants start to grow.

There may be lakes of hot water and holes where hot water spouts up high into the air.

The volcanoes are long dead, but might they erupt again?

Using the heat

Long after volcanoes have stopped erupting, the rocks below the ground are still very hot.

Water comes steaming up to the surface. In some places it is piped to nearby towns and used for heating.

In other places, natural steam is used to make electricity.

Good farmland

One of the reasons people live near volcanoes is because the land is so good for growing crops.

When the land is covered by
volcanic dust or lava, plants are
buried or burned by the heat.
But when they have weathered,
they make good farmland.

27

Volcano words

ash Bits of lava, rock and dust which some volcanoes spray into the air.

fumarole A hole in the side of a volcano where gas and fumes leak out into the air.

geothermal energy The name given to the energy in hot water pools caused by volcanic rocks. People use this energy for heating and making electricity.

lava Liquid rock flowing over the land outside a volcano. This slowly cools and becomes solid.

magma Liquid rock under the ground below a volcano.

plug Rock that sets hard in the mouth of a volcano. Sometimes volcanoes explode blowing away the top of the mountain.

vent The mouth of a volcano.

29

Index

Aa
air 15
animals 6
ash 28

Cc
cone 18
crater 19
crops 26

Dd
dust 12, 15, 27

Ee
Earth 6, 9, 13

earthquakes 14
electricity 25

Ff
farmland 26, 27
fumarole 28
fumes 20

Gg
gas 12
geothermal energy 28

Hh
heating 25
hot water 22, 25